THE RASTA COOKBOOK

THE
RASTA
COOKBOOK

Africa World Press, Inc.

P.O. Box 1892
Trenton, New Jersey 08607

Acknowledgements

The publisher and authors would like
to express thanks to all those who
have helped to make this book possible.

Illustrations

W. Stevenson (cover illustration)
Angela Wood (line illustrations)

Photography

Delroy Bent (photo *assorted fruits/veg*)
Wendy Stevenson (photo *shopping in Brixton*)
(photo *Market Scene in the Caribbean* —
Courtesy Tony Stone Photo Library)

Print Co-ordination

Daniel O'Brien

Design Concept

I. Osbourne

Typesetting

Galleon Photosetting, Ipswich

Africa World Press, Inc.
P.O. Box 1892
Trenton, NJ 08607

Copyright © Antillean Publishers Ltd., 1988

First Published by Antillean Publishers Ltd.,
1988

First Africa World Press Edition, 1992

Library of Congress Cataloging-in-Publication Data

The Rasta cookbook : vegetarian cusine, eaten with the salt of the
earth : recipes / compiled by Laura Osborne ; foreword by Ivor
Osbourne.
       p.   cm.
    ISBN 0-86543-133-7
    1. Vegetarian cookery. 2. Cookery, Tropical. 3. Ras Tafari
movement. I. Osborne, Laura.
TX837.R27 1992
641.5'636'09729--dc20
                                                      92-17760
                                                          CIP

Little has been written about the contribution of the Rastafari movement to the cultural tradition of the Caribbean people and until very recently little was known about the movement outside its place of origin, Jamaica. Yet as a cultural force, the movement has been gaining popularity at an immense rate over the last decade, despite the fact there has been very little written information disseminated.

There are now growing Rastafarian communities and numerous ethical converts to be seen in virtually every major metropolitan centre of the world, from New York to Tokyo. Rastafarians are in the main quite strikingly visible, their flowing tangled locks either cascading around their shoulders or confined within a beehive berets in the colour of the movement – red, gold, and green.

Red for the Blood
Green for the Earth
Gold for the Sun

Rastafarianism is a philosophy of nature.

Perhaps the first association that springs to mind at the mention of the word 'Rasta' is music, reggae music. Through the universal popularity of Reggae's greatest exponent, Bob Marley (now deceased), a devout rastafarian, Rasta music now has an audience in virtually every household in the western hemisphere.

To date the music of the Rastafari has been the most visible aspect of the movement outside Jamaica. Reggae music has perhaps gained a worldwide popularity for the sole reason of its simplicity of rhythm, part of a universal natural harmony akin to the heartbeat.

Rasta music is the music of nature, the sound of drums. Like the music, the food of the Rastafarian excels because of its simplicity. It is natural, '**Ital**'. It is simply vital.

The Rastafarian diet is essentially a vegetarian diet, but within the movement there are various factions, some who extend the diet to include either white meat, fish or shellfish as their interpretations of the philosophical base of the movement allows.

There are few excepted foods in Rasta cuisine, the most notable being pork. Pork products and derivatives are shunned by all Rastafari. The reason being drawn from the Macabee (coptic) version of the bible, the interpretation of which provides the cornerstone of Rastafari philosophy and world outlook.

The pages of this book are but an attempt to present some of the more popular recipes of Rastafarian tradition. As with all recipes there are variations as dictated by regionality and availability of ingredients; equally the recipes here can be varied to suit personal tastes.

The core of each recipe is based on ingredients commonly available in Jamaica, hence they are largely comprised of tropical fruit or vegetables. Modifications have been made however to account for seasonality and the more limited availability of some ingredients in more temperate climes by inclusion or suggestion of substitutes of a so similar nature and taste as to make as little difference as possible.

Again, this is not to say that one must adhere rigidly to the formulation of the dishes as presented in each recipe.

Rasta is the philosophy of freedom

Chop and change, substitute and experience

The only provision is that any substitute used must be of a natural, organic origin. If this is so, each variation of the prescribed recipe will provide as unique, fresh and natural an experience as the original recipe itself.

Market scene in the Caribbean.

YOU ARE WHAT YOU EAT

Nowhere is the belief that we are what we eat held more steadfastly than among the brethren of the Rastafari. There is good reason to shun additives, preservatives, all processed foods, all that is generally eaten which has no direct root in nature. For this reason the Rastafari always cook without added salt, a practice commonly known as 'Ital'.

TO BE IRIE IS TO BE AT ONE WITH NATURE

The state of being at one with nature, being at peace with oneself, with all the things around us is of the highest states. This is the natural high, and as it derives in music and chant, so it derives in good health and vitality, in the nature of the food we eat, the fruits and vegetables, the spices and the herbs.

ITAL IS VITAL

In Rasta cooking the natural flavour of each dish is embellished through the use of spices and herbs which compliment the natural essence of the ingredients. All care should be taken to preserve the natural purity of ingredients used in the preparation of 'Ital' food. This caring should extend from the preparation and serving, to eating. For this reason the devout brethren of the Rastafari will use only utensils made from natural materials, stone, earthenware. The matching of herbs or spice with vegetable is the result of a long and skilfully laid tradition originating from the African ancestry and cultural heritage of the Rastafari.

The herbs and spices are also fruits of the earth and are as such essential ingredients to the diet of the vital man.

The most widely used of the spices is pepper, fresh ripe peppers. The most piquant of the spices.

The most widely used herb is marijuana, use of which is prohibited by law in the UK and a number of other countries. It is, however, the strongest of the herbs, and in the tradition of the Rastafari unlimited by dish. It sweetens and embellishes all, baked, boiled, fried or stewed.

The spirit of Rasta is everywhere. As western man has set himself against the many essentials of the nature from which he was born, so he yearns to find peace with the world, to arrest the destruction of things which are natural, of himself.

Where better to halt the destruction but at the point where the body interfaces with nature, with the food we eat.

Eat Rasta

1988

Shopping day in
Brixton, London.

Key to Photo inset

1. Cho-Cho
2. Cocoes
3. Oranges
4. Breadfruit
5. Papaya
6. Sweet potato
7. Sweet Pepper
8. Corn (maize)
9. Thyme
10. Pumkin
11. Okra (Ladies Fingers)
12. Negro yam
13. Mangoes
14. Plantain (ripe)
15. Avocado
16. Spring onions
17. Hot peppers
18. Coconut
19. Grapefruits
20. Limes
21. Green bananas
22. Yellow yam

CONTENTS

DRINKS

Banana Punch

Carrot Punch

Coconut Punch

Ginger Drink

Mango Nectar

Paw Paw Orange Drink

Peanut Punch

Pineapple Cordial

Banana Punch

(Sweetie Come Brush Me)

Ingredients

4 ripe bananas
¾ pt (450 ml) water
¼ pt (150 ml) evaporated milk*
¼ tsp freshly grated nutmeg
3–4 drops of vanilla essence
honey

Method

Peel the bananas. Mash them with a fork and pass the purée through a fine sieve or liquidize with an electric blender. Add the water, evaporated milk, vanilla and nutmeg. Sweeten to taste with honey. Chill before serving.

Serves 3–4

A delicious drink, smooth and delicately spiced.

*NB. Soya milk can be used as substitute.

Carrot Punch

(Zion Juice)

Ingredients

1 lb (450 g) carrots
1 pt (550 ml) water
1 pt (550 ml) milk or soya milk
3 tbs condensed milk
1 tsp rosewater
½ tsp freshly grated nutmeg
molasses or raw cane sugar

Method

Peel and finely grate the carrots. Add the grated carrots to the water. Strain the mixture through a sieve lined with muslin, gathering up the muslin once the liquid has drained through and squeezing to extract all the juice. Repeat this process finally discarding the carrots. Stir the milk, condensed milk, rosewater and nutmeg into the carrot liquid. Add molasses or raw cane sugar to taste.

Serves 4–6

Coconut Punch

(Paradise Punch)

Ingredients

1 mature coconut
1½ pt (850 ml) water
4 oz (115 g) raw cane sugar
½ tsp almond essence

Method

Shell the coconut, peel and finely grate the flesh. Mix the grated coconut with the water and strain the mixture through a sieve lined with muslin, squeezing the muslin to extract all the juice. Discard the coconut. Add the raw cane sugar to the coconut liquid and stir until the sugar has dissolved. Flavour with almond essence and chill.

Serves 3–4

A subtly flavoured coconut drink, best served with ice.

Peanut Punch

(Governors Punch)

Ingredients

8 oz (225 g) shelled roasted peanuts
1½ pt (850 ml) water
½ pt (300 ml) evaporated milk or soya milk
½ tsp vanilla essence
½ tsp freshly grated nutmeg
raw cane sugar

Method

Place the shelled peanuts in an electric blender or food processor. Measure out 1 pt (550 ml) of the water and gradually pour this into the blender while grinding the peanuts. Leave the blender running for 1–2 minutes until the peanuts are thoroughly blended. Strain the mixture through a sieve lined with muslin, pouring in a little at a time and squeezing the muslin to extract all the liquid. After squeezing discard the contents of the muslin. Repeat until all the peanut mixture is used up. Add milk, then sweeten the drink to taste with cane sugar and flavour with vanilla essence and grated nutmeg.

Serves 3–4

Ginger Drink

Ingredients

1 lb (450 g) fresh root ginger
3 pt (1650 ml) water
1 lb (450 g) raw cane sugar
juice of 2 limes

Method

Thinly peel the fresh ginger, grate and mix with the water in a large saucepan. Bring to the boil and simmer for 3–4 minutes. Cover the pan, turn off the heat and leave for at least 24 hours. Strain the liquid through a sieve. Add the lime juice and stir in the raw cane sugar until thoroughly dissolved. Chill.

Serves 6–8

Note: This drink is best left to mature for a day before drinking. It is most refreshing served cold with plenty of ice.

Mango Nectar

(Sunsplash)

Ingredients

3 ripe medium-sized mangoes
juice of 1 lime
1½ pt (550 ml) water
raw cane sugar

Method

Peel the mangoes, cut the flesh from the central stone and either rub through a fine sieve or liquidize in an electric blender. Add to the mango purée, the lime juice and water. Add sufficient raw cane sugar to sweeten, stirring the mixture until the sugar has dissolved. Chill and serve.

Serves 3–4

A tropical flavoured drink, fresh orange or pineapple can be added for a more exotic blend of flavours.

Pawpaw Orange Drink

(Yellow Bird)

Ingredients

1 ripe pawpaw
½ pt (275 ml) orange juice
juice of 1 lime
2 pt (1100 ml) water
4 oz (115 g) raw cane sugar

Method

Peel the pawpaw, cut it in half, scoop out and discard the black seeds. Roughly chop the flesh and liquidize in an electric blender until a smooth purée is produced. Mix the pawpaw with the orange juice, lime juice and water. Stir in the raw cane sugar until it is dissolved. Chill.

Serves 4–6

Pineapple Cordial

Ingredients

1 ripe pineapple
4–5 slices peeled root ginger
3 whole cloves
2 limes
2 pt (1100 ml) boiling water
4 oz (115 g) raw cane sugar

Method

Peel the pineapple thickly and reserve the flesh for use in another dish. Crush the slices of root ginger and thinly slice the limes. Place the pineapple peel, ginger, limes and whole cloves in a large bowl. Pour on the boiling water, cover and allow to steep for 24 hours. Strain the liquid discarding the pineapple peel, limes and spices. Stir in the raw cane sugar until dissolved. Chill.

Serves 4–6

An excellent way of using fresh pineapple trimmings. This is a refreshing ginger flavoured drink and can be served with ice and garnished with slices of lime.

SNACKS/APPETIZERS

Akkra

Plantain Cakes

Plantain Chips

Almond Dip

Avocado Dip

Aubergine Fritters

Carrot Fritters

Cornmeal Fritters

Fried Ripe Bananas

Ital Omelette

Tomato Filled Avocado

Akkra

(Bean Cakes)

Ingredients

½ lb (225 g) black-eyed beans
1 hot pepper
vegetable oil for frying

Method

Cover the black-eyed beans with plenty of cold water and leave to soak overnight. Drain. Rub the outer skin off the beans and discard. Cover the beans with more cold water and soak for a further 2–3 hours. Prepare the Creole sauce (see page 81). Drain the beans and grind in small amounts in an electric blender. Cut the hot pepper in half, remove the seeds and chop finely. Add the pepper to the beans and beat the mixture until very light. Heat the oil in a heavy frying pan and drop in tablespoons of the mixture. Fry the beancakes on both sides until golden brown. Serve with Creole sauce.

Serves 4

These piquant bean cakes need a little advance planning as allowance must be made for soaking times. They are, nevertheless, simple to cook and are good served very hot with a spicy sauce.

Note: Care should always be taken to wash hands and utensils after preparing hot peppers.

Plantain Cakes

Ingredients

3 ripe plantains
½ tsp baking powder
1 tbs raw cane sugar
vegetable oil for frying

Method

Bring a large pan of water to the boil. Cut the ends off the plantains, place the plantains in the water and cook until soft. Drain. When they are cool enough to handle peel the plantains, mash them well with a fork and mix in the baking powder and sugar. Shape the mixture into small cakes. Heat the vegetable oil in a heavy frying pan and fry the cakes on both sides until golden.

Serves 4

Plantain Chips

Ingredients

3 green plantains
juice of 3 limes
vegetable oil for frying

Method

To peel the plantains, slice the ends off and cut each plantain in two. Deeply score the skin with a knife cutting right through to the flesh down the length of the plantains. Slide your fingertip under the skin and peel it away horizontally rather than lengthways. Now slice the plantains diagonally very thinly. Soak the slices in lime juice for 10–15 minutes. Dry thoroughly. Heat the oil in a frying pan and when hot fry the plantain chips until crisp and golden brown.

Serves 4

Plantain chips may be eaten as a snack or served with a vegetable dip as an unusual first course.

Almond Dip

Ingredients

2 oz (55 g) whole almonds
2 medium tomatoes
¼ pt (150 ml) peanut oil
juice of ½ lime
1 clove garlic
freshly ground black pepper

Method

Preheat the oven to 180 degrees C. (gas 4). Blanch the almonds in boiling water for 2–3 minutes. Remove the skins from the nuts and toast on a baking tray in a hot oven until lightly browned. Skin and de-seed the tomatoes. Place the skinned tomatoes, the almonds, garlic and lime juice in an electric blender and blend until the mixture forms a smooth paste. Add the peanut oil gradually, with the blender still running, pouring it in a thin stream until it is completely absorbed and the dip is thick and creamy. Season with freshly ground black pepper.

Serves 4

Avocado Dip

Ingredients

2 large ripe avocados
1–2 spring onions
juice of ½ lime

Method

Halve the avocados, remove the seed and scoop out the flesh. Finely chop the spring onions. Put the avocados and the lime juice in a blender or food processor and blend until smooth. Stir the chopped spring onions into the avocado mixture.

Serves 4

Serve either of these dips with plantain chips or a selection of fresh raw vegetables, celery, cauliflower, carrots, cucumber, peppers sliced lengthways into sticks or divided into florets.

Aubergine Fritters

Ingredients

1 large aubergine
1 clove garlic : 2 tbs milk
3 oz (85 g) wholemeal flour
1 tsp baking powder : ¼ tsp paprika
freshly ground black pepper
vegetable oil for frying

Method

Bring a large pan of water to the boil and cook the aubergine whole until tender. Halve the cooked aubergine, scoop the flesh from the skin and either rub through a sieve or mash with a fork until a purée is formed. Finely chop the garlic and add to the aubergine purée together with the milk. Stir in the flour and baking powder and season with paprika and black pepper. The mixture should have a fairly stiff consistency. Heat the vegetable oil in a frying pan and when hot drop tablespoons of the aubergine mixture into the oil. Fry on both sides until golden.

Serves 4

These simply made fritters have a nutty flavour and can be served with a hot spicy sauce or garnished with salad.

Carrot Fritters

(Floyd's Fritters)

Ingredients

3 medium-sized carrots
4 oz (115 g) wholemeal flour
½ tsp baking powder
¼ tsp ground cinnamon
¼ tsp freshly grated nutmeg
3 oz (85 g) raw cane sugar
2–3 tbs milk or soya milk
vegetable oil for frying

Method

Peel and grate the carrots. Sift the flour, baking powder and spices into a bowl. Add the sugar and mix in the grated carrot. Pour on the milk a spoonful at a time stirring the ingredients to produce a soft dropping consistency. The mixture should not be too wet. Heat the vegetable oil in a heavy frying pan. Drop tablespoons of the carrot mixture into the oil and fry until the fritters are golden brown on both sides. Serve hot.

Serves 4

These are delicately spiced sweet fritters, one of my father's own recipes.

Cornmeal fritters

(The Herb Fritters)

Ingredients

2 oz (55 g) cornmeal
2 oz (55 g) wholemeal flour
½ tsp baking powder
¼ pt (150 ml) coconut milk
½ medium onion : 2 spring onions
½ hot pepper : ½ tsp fresh thyme
2–3 mint leaves : vegetable oil for frying

Method

Mix the cornmeal, flour and baking powder together in a bowl. Gradually stir in the milk until the mixture is smooth. Peel and finely chop the onion, chop the spring onions, de-seed and finely chop the hot pepper. Add these ingredients to the cornmeal mixture together with the thyme and chopped mint leaves. Heat the vegetable oil in a frying pan and drop in tablespoons of the mixture. When one side is golden brown turn them over and fry the other side.

Serves 4

A delicious savoury fritter flavoured with onions and fresh herbs.

Note: Care should always be taken to wash hands and utensils directly after preparing hot peppers.

Fried Ripe Bananas

(Sweet Start)

Ingredients

6 firm ripe bananas
2 tbs cornmeal
2 tbs coconut milk
3 tbs vegetable oil

Method

Peel the ripe bananas and slice them in half lengthways. Coat the banana halves with the cornmeal, pressing the cornmeal on gently. Heat the vegetable oil in a heavy frying pan over a medium heat. When the oil is hot, quickly dip the banana halves in the coconut milk and then transfer to the frying pan. Fry until golden brown, turning frequently.

Serves 4

Ital Omelette

Ingredients

4 green bananas
1 medium-sized onion
½ pt (275 ml) water
1 tbs wholemeal flour
½ tsp freshly grated nutmeg
3 tbs vegetable oil

Method

Slice the ends off the bananas and cut them in half crossways. Using a sharp knife slit through the skin to the flesh along the length of each banana half. Prise off the skin using your fingers. Place the bananas in an electric blender or food processor and blend until smooth adding the water a little at a time to produce a soft consistency. In a bowl, mix the bananas with the peeled and finely chopped onion. Stir in the wholemeal flour and nutmeg. Heat the vegetable oil in a heavy frying pan, pour in the banana mixture and fry on both sides until golden brown. Divide into portions and serve garnished with salad.

Serves 4

Tomato Filled Avocado

Ingredients

1 lb (450 g) tomatoes
¼ pt (150 g) mayonnaise
¼ pt (150 g) sour cream or yoghurt
2 slices peeled root ginger
freshly ground black pepper
juice of ½ lime
2 large avocados

Method

Blanch and peel the tomatoes, reserving one or two for a garnish. Coarsely chop the peeled tomatoes, liquidize in a blender and press through a sieve to produce a smooth purée. Beat the mayonnaise and yoghurt into the tomatoes. Finely chop the slices of fresh ginger and add to the mixture together with a seasoning of black pepper and lime juice. Halve the avocados and remove the stone. Heap the tomato mixture into the centre of each avocado half and garnish with slices of tomato.

Serves 4

Eggless mayonnaise or soya-based alternatives can be substituted in this dish.

SOUPS

Ackee Soup

Cold Avocado Soup

Creamed Breadfruit Soup

Curried Lentil Soup with Coconut

Peanut or Groundnut Soup

Pumpkin and Cho Cho Soup

Red Bean Soup

Callaloo Soup

Ital Soup

Sweetcorn Soup

Ackee Soup

Ingredients

1 large tin ackees (20 oz or 550 g)
1 pt (550 ml) vegetable stock
2 medium-sized tomatoes
1 hot pepper
2 spring onions
freshly ground black pepper

Method

Empty the tin of ackees into a large saucepan and add the vegetable stock. Blanch and peel the tomatoes and roughly chop. Slice the spring onions. Add the tomatoes, spring onions and the whole hot pepper to the saucepan, season with freshly ground black pepper and bring to the boil. Simmer the soup on a gentle heat for 20–25 minutes. Remove the hot pepper from the pan, then liquidize the soup in an electric blender. Return to the saucepan and reheat. Serve sprinkled with paprika.

Serves 4

Here Jamaica's national food is used as the basis for a light peppery soup.

Chilled Avocado Soup

Ingredients

3 ripe avocados
juice of ½ lime
1½ pt (850 ml) milk
4–5 mint leaves
freshly ground black pepper

Method

Halve the avocados, remove the seed and scoop out the flesh. Mash the avocados with the lime juice to make a purée, transfer to an electric blender and blend the avocado mixture at the same time gradually pouring in the milk. Liquidize until the ingredients are thoroughly blended. Stir in the chopped mint leaves and season with freshly ground black pepper. Chill until ready to serve.

Serves 4

A beautiful green soup which is served refreshingly chilled for a hot summer day.

Creamed Breadfruit Soup

(Manna Soup)

Ingredients

2 medium-sized onions : 2 cloves garlic
½ lb (225 g) breadfruit : 2 tbs vegetable oil
1 bayleaf : 1½ pt (850 ml) vegetable stock
½ pt (300 ml) milk
freshly ground black pepper
spring onion tops or parsley

Method

Peel the garlic cloves and chop finely. Using a sharp knife peel the skin from the breadfruit and remove the core. Chop the breadfruit into dice. Heat the vegetable oil in a large saucepan and sauté the onion and garlic until soft but not coloured. Add the diced breadfruit, bayleaf and vegetable stock. Bring to the boil, cover the pan and simmer on a low heat until the breadfruit is tender. Remove the bayleaf and liquidize the soup in an electric blender or press through a fine sieve. Return the soup to the pan, add the milk and season with black pepper. Reheat gently taking care not to boil then serve sprinkled with chopped spring onion tops or fresh parsley.

Serves 4

Curried Lentil Soup with Coconut

Ingredients

1 medium-sized onion : 2 cloves garlic
2 slices peeled root ginger : 1 small red pepper
1 small green pepper : 2 tbs vegetable oil
2 tsp ground coriander : 1 tsp ground cummin
1 tsp garam masala : 2 oz (55g) creamed coconut
1¾ pt (1 ltr) vegetable stock : 4 oz (115 g) split red lentils
1 hot pepper : freshly ground black pepper

Method

Peel and chop the onion. Crush the peeled cloves of garlic and the slices of ginger together using a pestle and mortar, adding a little water to produce a thick paste. Slice the red and green peppers into strips. Heat the vegetable oil in a large saucepan, add the chopped onion and fry on a medium heat until transparent. Add the garlic and ginger paste and fry for two minutes before putting in the spices. Fry the spices for another minute then stir in the red and green peppers. Roughly grate the creamed coconut into the pan and stir until it has blended to make a thick sauce. Add the vegetable stock, the washed lentils, the whole hot pepper and black pepper. Simmer the soup for 35–40 minutes. Stir occasionally being careful not to crush the hot pepper. Remove the hot pepper before serving.

Serves 4

Peanut or Groundnut Soup

(Ital Nut Soup)

Ingredients

4 oz (115 g) shelled roasted peanuts
1¾ pt (1 ltr) vegetable stock
3–4 pimento berries
¼ pt (150 ml) evaporated milk
freshly ground black pepper
¼ tsp paprika or dash hot pepper sauce

Method

Shell the peanuts and place them in an electric blender. Grind the nuts in the blender, adding a little vegetable stock to make a smooth paste. When the peanuts are thoroughly ground pour the contents of the blender into a saucepan. Mix in the rest of the stock, add the pimento berries and freshly ground black pepper. Bring to the boil and cook on a low heat for 15 minutes. Stir in the evaporated milk and cook gently for a further few minutes. Season to taste with paprika or hot pepper sauce. Remove the pimento berries before serving.

Serves 4

An unusual soup delicately flavoured with peppers and pimento.

Pumpkin and Cho Cho Soup

Ingredients

1 lb (450 g) pumpkin
1 cho cho : 1½ pt (800 ml) water
2 medium-sized tomatoes
1 spring onion : 1 sprig thyme
1 small blade mace
freshly ground black pepper
¼ pt (150 ml) coconut milk

Method

Peel and wash the pumpkin, remove the seeds and chop into 2 cm dice. Peel the cho cho, cut into quarters lengthways and remove the heart. Dice. Place the pumpkin and the cho cho in a saucepan with the water and simmer on a medium heat for 15 minutes until cooked. Meanwhile peel and chop the tomatoes and slice the spring onion into fine rounds. Add these to the saucepan together with the thyme, mace, ground black pepper and coconut milk. Simmer for a further 15 minutes then remove the thyme before serving.

Serves 4

Here the vegetables cook down to produce a richly flavoured golden soup.

Red Bean Soup

Ingredients

1 lb (450 g) red kidney beans
2 pt (1100 ml) water : 1 large onion
1 medium-sized carrot : 1 stick celery
1 green pepper : 2 tbs vegetable oil
2 cloves garlic : 1 hot pepper
1 sprig thyme : freshly ground black pepper

Method

Soak the kidney beans overnight in plenty of cold water. Drain, place in a large saucepan with 2 pt (1100 ml) fresh water and simmer covered for 1½ hours until the beans are very tender. Peel and finely chop the onion, peel and slice the carrot, chop the celery and green pepper. In a separate pan heat the vegetable oil, add the chopped vegetables and the crushed cloves of garlic and cook gently until soft. Crush some of the cooked kidney beans with their liquid to make a coarse purée. Add this and the remaining beans to the pan with the whole hot pepper, thyme and black pepper. Simmer for 20 minutes. Remove thyme and whole pepper before serving.

Serves 4

The combination of red beans and different coloured vegetables makes this a visually attractive as well as a nourishing soup.

Callaloo Soup

(Illaloo Soup)

Ingredients

1 lb (450 g) callaloo leaves : 1 aubergine
2 green bananas : 1 large onion
2 cloves garlic : 1½ pts (850 ml) water
4 pimento berries : 3 whole cloves
1 sprig thyme : 1 hot pepper
freshly ground black pepper : ½ lb (225 g) young okra
¼ pt (150 ml) coconut milk

Method

Thoroughly wash the callaloo leaves and remove most of the stem. Drain and coarsely chop. Peel the aubergine and chop into 2 cm dice. Keeping the skin on, chop the green bananas into thick slices. Place these vegetables together with chopped onion and garlic in a large saucepan. Add the water, pimento, cloves, thyme, hot pepper and freshly ground black pepper. Bring the soup to the boil and simmer, covered until the vegetables are tender. Take out the slices of green banana, remove the skin and return to the pan. Remove the hot pepper which should still be whole and the thyme. Rub the soup through a sieve or liquidize briefly. Slice the okra into rounds. Return the soup to the pan, add the okra and coconut milk and cook for a further 10 minutes. Adjust the seasoning and serve.

Serves 4

Spinach, if more readily available, can be used as a substitute for callaloo. With a salad and wholemeal bread this soup becomes a meal in itself.

Ital Soup

Ingredients

1 lb (450 g) yam : ½ lb (225 g) sweet potato
1 lb (450 g) pumpkin : 1 lb (450 g) callaloo
½ small cabbage : ½ lb (225 g) carrots
1 cho cho : 1 green pepper
2 cloves garlic : 2 medium-sized tomatoes
3 spring onions : 2 pts (1100 ml) water

Method

First prepare the vegetables. Peel the yam, sweet potato and pumpkin and cut into large die, removing the seeds from the pumpkin. Carefully wash the callaloo, trimming away any thick stems and chop. Coarsely chop the cabbage having carefully discarded the outer leaves, peel and slice the carrots. Peel the cho cho, cut it lengthways into quarters and remove the heart. Roughly dice the cho cho and green pepper, peel and chop the tomatoes and slice the spring onions. Place the pumpkin and root vegetables in a large saucepan with the water. Bring to the boil and simmer for 10 minutes. Add to the pan the callaloo, cabbage, cho cho, pepper and finally the chopped tomatoes and spring onions. Season with plenty of freshly ground black pepper and simmer for twenty minutes more until cooked.

Serves 4–6

A substantial soup that will satisfy the largest of appetites; a true "Ital" feast which requires only fresh fruit juice to complete the meal.

Sweetcorn Soup

Ingredients

8 oz (225 g) sweetcorn : 1½ pt (850 ml) water
⅓ pt (200 ml) coconut milk : 2 medium-sized potatoes
1 lb (450 g) pumpkin : 1 stick celery
2 spring onions : 1 medium-sized tomato
1 sprig thyme
freshly ground black pepper
juice of ½ lime

Method

Place the corn in a heavy based saucepan, cover with water, bring to the boil and simmer. Meanwhile peel the potatoes and pumpkin remove the pumpkin seeds and dice both vegetables. Chop the celery and spring onions, peel and chop the tomato. Add the coconut milk to the pan together with the prepared vegetables. Season with thyme and freshly ground black pepper and add the lime juice. Continue to cook on a low heat for 20–25 minutes until the vegetables are soft. Remove the thyme before serving.

Serves 4

A rich vegetable soup thickened with potato and pumpkin. Serve with a simple salad or wholemeal bread.

DUMPLINGS
AND ROTI

Cornmeal Dumplings

Herb Dumplings

Fried Dumplings

Roti

Cornmeal Dumplings

Ingredients

2 oz (55 g) cornmeal
2 oz (55 g) wholemeal flour
1 tsp baking powder
knob of unsalted butter or vegetable margarine
cold water

Method

Sift the cornmeal, wholemeal flour and baking powder into a bowl. Rub in the unsalted butter or vegetable margarine. Add sufficient cold water, a little at a time, to form a soft dough. Knead briefly on a floured board or worktop. Divide the dough into equal portions and shape into dumplings. Add to soup or cook in plenty of boiling water for 10–12 minutes until done.

Makes approximately 6

The addition of baking powder gives the dumplings a lighter texture. If however you prefer the firmer variety simply reduce the amount of baking powder or omit altogether.

Herb Dumplings

Ingredients

4 oz (115 g) wholemeal flour
½ oz (15 g) vegetable margarine
1 tsp baking powder
1 tsp fresh chives
1 tsp fresh thyme
1 tsp fresh coriander
cold water

Method

Sift the flour and baking powder into a bowl. Rub in the vegetable margarine until well blended. Finely chop the fresh herbs and add to the mixture together with sufficient cold water to bind the ingredients and produce a soft dough. Lightly knead the dough on a floured surface until smooth. Divide the mixture, shape into dumplings and drop them into soup or boiling water. Cook for about 10 minutes.

Makes approximately 6

Dumplings need not be round or sphere-like in shape. They can be pressed into flat rounds of varying sizes; or rolled between the hands into long fingers known as "spinners". Round, long, fat or skinny, shape them as you please.

Fried Dumplings

(Johnny Cakes)

Ingredients

8 oz (225 g) wholemeal flour
1½ tsp baking powder
½ oz (15 g) unsalted butter or vegetable margarine
cold water
vegetable oil for frying

Method

Sift the flour and baking powder together. Rub in the butter or vegetable margarine until well blended. Gradually add cold water to the mixture until the ingredients bind to form a stiff dough. Knead the dough on a floured surface until smooth. Divide the mixture, shape into balls and flatten slightly. Heat the vegetable oil in a heavy frying pan and fry the dumplings until brown on both sides.

Makes approximately 8

The only type of dumpling that is not cooked in soup or boiling water. Fried dumplings are often eaten as a snack and were perhaps a popular take-away meal, hence another alternative name, "Journey cakes".

Roti

Ingredients

8 oz (225 g) wholemeal flour
1 tbs cornmeal
1 tsp baking powder
1½ oz (40 g) unsalted butter or vegetable margarine
cold water
vegetable oil

Method

Sift the flour, cornmeal and baking powder into a bowl. Rub in the butter or vegetable margarine. Add the cold water, a tablespoon at a time to bind the dough (it should not be sticky). Knead until smooth. Cover the dough and leave in a warm place for half an hour. Knead again for 3–4 minutes and divide into four equal portions. On a floured surface roll out the portions into thin rounds. Lightly brush each one with a little vegetable oil, roll all of them into a ball again and leave to rest, covered, for 15 minutes. Roll out again into thin 8-inch (20 cm) circles. Heat a heavy frying pan. Brush one side of the roti with vegetable oil and cook for 1 minute. Coat the other side with oil, turn it over and cook for another minute. Repeat this process turning the roti frequently until brown. Wrap in a towel to keep warm until the other roti are cooked.

A flat pancake like bread made with a mixture of cornmeal and wholemeal flour.

MAIN COURSES

Baked Sweet Potatoes

Breadfruit in Coconut Sauce

Callaloo with Vegetables

Cou Cou with Okra

Mixed Rice with Vegetables

Okra and Aubergine ● Sweetcorn and Rice

Curried Ackees ● Pumpkin Curry

Cashew Nut Patties ● Fried Yam Cakes

Millet and Tofu Patties ● Black Bean Stew

Ital Stew ● Lentil Stew

Millet and Spinach Stew ● Stewed Ackees

Vegetable Stew with Cornmeal Dumplings

Aubergine Stuffed with Cashew Nuts

Stuffed Red Peppers

Baked Sweet Potatoes

Ingredients

2 lb (900 g) sweet potatoes
2 oz (55 g) unsalted butter or vegetable margarine
juice of ½ orange
freshly ground black pepper
2–3 firm tomatoes

Method

Carefully wash the sweet potatoes and boil in their skins in plenty of water for 20–25 minutes until soft. Drain. When cool enough to handle remove the skins and rub the potatoes through a sieve. Mix 1 oz (25 g) of the butter into the sweet potato purée together with the orange juice. Lightly season with freshly ground black pepper. Butter a shallow baking dish and spread the mixture evenly in it. Top with sliced tomatoes and dot with remaining butter. Bake in a preheated oven at 180 degrees C. for 20 minutes.

Serves 4

The sweetness of the potato combines well with a sharp citrus flavour to create an unusual tasting dish. Serve with a salad or green vegetable.

Breadfruit in Coconut Sauce

(Breadfruit Run Down)

Ingredients

½ breadfruit
1 medium-sized onion
2 medium-sized tomatoes
2 tbs vegetable oil
1 bayleaf
1 sprig thyme
freshly ground black pepper
¾ pt (425 ml) coconut milk

Method

Using a sharp knife slice the breadfruit into thick wedges. Peel the breadfruit and cut out the heart. Peel and chop the onion and tomatoes. Heat the vegetable oil in a saucepan, add the onion and fry until soft but not brown. Add the chopped tomatoes, bayleaf, thyme and freshly ground black pepper. Stir in the coconut milk and bring the liquid to the boil. Add the breadfruit, cover the pan and simmer on a gentle heat for 30 minutes or until the breadfruit is tender.

Serves 4

The nutty flavour of the breadfruit is complemented in this recipe by a rich coconut sauce with a subtle accent of fresh herbs. Serve with plainly cooked green vegetables and fried dumplings.

Callaloo with Vegetables

(Illaloo Feast)

Ingredients

1 lb (450 g) callaloo : 1 lb (450 g) pak choy or chinese cabbage
1 medium-sized onion : 2 spring onions
2 medium-sized tomatoes : 3 tbs vegetable oil
1 tsp fresh thyme : 1 hot pepper
freshly ground black pepper : 1 tin ackees

Method

Thoroughly wash the callaloo and pak choy or chinese cabbage. Trim away the thicker stems and roughly chop. Peel and slice the onion, slice the spring onions, blanch and peel the tomatoes then chop them. Heat the vegetable oil in a heavy saucepan, add the sliced onion and cook until soft. Toss in the chopped greens together with the spring onions, thyme, whole hot pepper and black pepper. Cover the pan, turn the heat to minimum and cook, stirring occasionally for 15–20 minutes. Do not let the mixture dry out during this time and be careful when stirring not to break the whole hot pepper. Meanwhile drain the tin of ackees and steam gently over a pan of boiling water. When the vegetables are cooked remove the hot pepper and carefully stir in the ackees.

Serves 4

The callaloo may be substituted by fresh spinach which is more widely available in Britain. The dish may be served with rice or roti and an accompaniment such as fried plantain.

Cou Cou with Okra

(Turn Cornmeal)

Ingredients

½ lb (225 g) young okra
1 medium-sized onion
1¾ pts (1 ltr) water
freshly ground black pepper
1 tsp fresh thyme
6 oz (170 g) cornmeal
1 oz (25 g) unsalted butter

Method

Wash the okra, cut off the stems and slice into thin rounds. Peel and finely chop the onion. Place the okra and onion in a pan, cover with water and season with freshly ground black pepper and thyme. Bring to the boil and simmer covered for 10 minutes until the okra is cooked. Pour the measured cornmeal into the pan in a steady stream, stirring constantly. Continue to cook until the mixture is thick and smooth (about 10 minutes) spoon the mixture into a greased dish to mould and turn out onto a warm serving plate, spreading the butter on top. Alternatively serve directly without moulding.

Serves 4

Serve with freshly cooked vegetables or a salad. If any of the cou cou is left over it is also good sliced and then fried in a little vegetable oil or butter.

Mixed Rice and Vegetables

Ingredients

6 oz (170 g) red kidney beans
½ pt (275 ml) coconut milk
8 oz (225 g) pumpkin : 2 medium-sized carrots
1 medium-sized onion : 2 spring onions
freshly ground black pepper
½ tsp fresh thyme : 8 oz (225 g) brown rice

Method

Soak the red kidney beans in plenty of cold water overnight. Drain, cover with fresh water and boil for 1 hour or until tender, adding the coconut milk towards the end of the cooking. Peel the pumpkin, remove the seeds and dice. Peel and slice the carrots, onion and spring onions. Add the vegetables to the pan, stir in the seasoning of black pepper and fresh thyme. Finally add the washed rice and top up the liquid level in the pan with water to come about 1–2 cm above the vegetables and rice. Bring to the boil, cover tightly and simmer on a low heat for 20–25 minutes, checking from time to time and adding more water if necessary.

Serves 4

A one pot meal, this is a very filling dish and is best served with a simple salad.

Okra and Aubergine

(Gumbo)

Ingredients

1 large aubergine : ½ lb (225 g) okra
1 hot pepper : 1 medium-sized onion
1 clove garlic : 1 green pepper
2 tbs vegetable oil
1 lb (450 g) tomatoes
freshly ground black pepper

Method

Peel and dice the aubergine. Trim the stems from the okra and slice into thick rounds. De-seed and finely chop the hot pepper, peel and slice the onion and garlic, slice the green pepper into strips. Heat the vegetable oil over a medium flame and cook the sliced onion and garlic until transparent. Add the green pepper, fry for two minutes longer, then add the aubergine, okra, hot pepper and the tomatoes which have been peeled and chopped. Season with freshly ground black pepper and let cook, covered on a low heat for 20–25 minutes, stirring occasionally.

Serves 4

An adaptation of a traditional creole dish, it combines the complementary tastes of aubergine, okra, tomato and sweet pepper. Serve with plainly cooked brown rice.

Note: Be careful to wash hands and utensils after preparing the hot pepper.

Sweetcorn and Rice

Ingredients

1 medium-sized onion
1 red pepper
8 oz (225 g) sweetcorn
1½ pts (850 ml) water
2 tbs vegetable oil
¼ pt (150 ml) coconut milk
freshly ground black pepper
8 oz (225 g) brown rice

Method

Peel and slice the onion, slice the red pepper into strips discarding the seeds. Place the sweetcorn in a saucepan with the water, bring to the boil and simmer. Meanwhile sauté the onion and red pepper in the vegetable oil over a medium heat until they are soft. Add them to the sweetcorn together with the coconut milk, the black pepper and the washed brown rice. Leave the cover off the pan and simmer gently for 20–30 minutes until the rice is soft and all the water has been absorbed.

Serves 4

Serve with fried plantain and a green vegetable such as steamed cho cho.

Curried Ackees

(Coolie Ackees)

Ingredients

1 medium-sized onion : 2 cloves garlic
3 slices fresh root ginger : 2 tbs vegetable oil
½ tsp black mustard seeds : 2 tsp ground coriander
1 tsp ground cummin : 1 tsp garam masala
¼ tsp turmeric : 1 medium-sized tomato
freshly ground black pepper : 1 tin ackees (20 oz or 550 g)

Method

Peel and fry the onion. Crush the peeled ginger and garlic into a paste using a pestle and mortar, adding a little water to moisten. Place the oil in a heavy based pan over a medium heat. Stir in the onion and fry for 3–4 minutes before adding the garlic and ginger paste. Keep frying until the onion begins to brown, then add the black mustard seeds and the spices in the order indicated. Fry the spices for 2–3 minutes. Finally add the peeled and chopped tomato and cook for a further 5 minutes adding warm water a tablespoon at a time to produce a thick sauce. Drain the ackees of most of their liquid and gently stir into the pan. Season with freshly ground black pepper and simmer for 5–6 minutes.

Serves 4

Garnish with fresh coriander if available. Serve with rice.

Note: When selecting ackees, if only tinned ones are available, select brands packed without preservatives.

Pumpkin Curry

Ingredients

1½ lb (675 g) pumpkin : 1 large potato
1 medium-sized onion : 1 clove garlic
2 tbs vegetable oil : 1 stick cinnamon (3 inch/7 cm)
3 whole cloves : 1 bayleaf
1 tsp cummin seeds : 2 tsp ground coriander
1 tsp garam masala
2 medium-sized tomatoes

Method

Peel and dice the pumpkin and potato into 1-inch (2 cm) cubes, having first removed the seeds from the pumpkin. Peel the onion and garlic and slice. Heat the vegetable oil in a pan and fry the onion and garlic until beginning to brown. Add the cinnamon stick, cloves, bayleaf and cummin seeds followed by the ground spices. Fry stirring for 2–3 minutes. Peel and coarsely chop the tomatoes and add to the pan. Stir in the chopped pumpkin and potato and cook on a low heat until the vegetables are tender. Stir occasionally to make sure the mixture does not stick, adding 2–3 tablespoons of water if necessary. Remove the cinnamon and bayleaf before serving.

Serves 4

A warm and spicy dish. Take care not to stir too vigorously while the dish is cooking so the vegetables do not disintegrate too much. Excellent with roti and a fresh salad.

Cashew Patties

Ingredients

3 oz (85 g) bulgar wheat
4 oz (115 g) carrots
1 medium-sized onion
3 oz (85 g) cashew nuts
2 tbs vegetable oil
1–2 tbs vegetable stock : freshly ground black pepper
wholemeal flour : vegetable oil for frying

Method

To prepare the bulgar wheat simply place in a bowl, pour on enough boiling water to cover and soak for about one hour. When ready to use take handfuls of the wheat and squeeze to extract excess water. Peel and grate the carrots, peel and finely chop the onion and chop the cashew nuts. Mix these ingredients into the bulgar wheat. Stir in the vegetable oil and enough vegetable stock to moisten the mixture if necessary (the mixture should not get too wet). Season with freshly ground black pepper. Divide the mixture and shape into patties with floured hands. Coat both sides of the patties with wholemeal flour, then fry in hot oil for 5–6 minutes each side until brown.

Serves 4

Use the unsalted cashews for this recipe. These patties are a little difficult to keep in shape while frying, but are nevertheless delicious. Serve with plenty of salad or cooked vegetables.

Fried Yam Cakes

(Fried Yatties)

Ingredients

2 lb (900 g) yam
1 oz (55 g) unsalted butter or vegetable margarine
1 medium-sized onion
2 tbs parsley
freshly ground black pepper
vegetable oil for frying

Method

Peel and wash the yam, cut into two pieces and boil until soft. Drain. Mash the cooked yam with the butter or vegetable margarine until smooth. Peel and finely chop the onion, chop the parsley. Stir the onion, parsley and freshly ground black pepper into the yam mixture. Place the vegetable oil in a heavy frying pan over a medium heat. When hot, drop in tablespoons of the mixture and fry until golden brown.

Serves 4

Very quick and easy to make these yam cakes can be served with a salad or vegetable accompaniments.

Millet and Tofu Patties

Ingredients

2 tbs vegetable oil : 1 medium-sized onion
1 clove garlic : 4 oz (115 g) millet grains
1 pt (550 ml) boiling water
4 oz (115 g) tofu : 1 hot pepper
1 tbs tomato purée : 1 tbs soya sauce or tamari
freshly ground black pepper
vegetable oil for frying

Method

Heat the vegetable oil in a saucepan. Peel and finely chop the onion and garlic and fry for 2–3 minutes. Stir in the millet grains frying until they are lightly coloured. Carefully pour on the boiling water and let the millet cook for 20 minutes. Drain and cool. Blend the millet and tofu together in an electric blender. De-seed and finely chop the hot pepper and stir into the mixture together with the tomato purée, soya sauce and black pepper. Chill thoroughly before dividing into 8 flatcakes. Shallow fry in hot oil on both sides until golden.

Serves 4

These savoury patties can be eaten "burger-like" in a wholemeal bun, or with freshly cooked vegetables.

Note: Hands and utensils should be thoroughly washed after preparing the hot pepper.

Black Bean Stew

Ingredients

1 lb (450 g) black beans : 1½ pts (850 ml) water
1 medium-sized onion : 2 cloves garlic
1 hot pepper : 1 green pepper
3 tbs vegetable oil : 2 bayleaves
½ tsp dried oregano : ½ tsp ground cummin
4 pimento berries : freshly ground black pepper
1 tsp raw cane sugar : 1 tbs cornflour

Method

Soak the black beans overnight in plenty of cold water. Drain. Place in a heavy saucepan with 1½ pts (850 ml) water and simmer, covered, for 1–1½ hours or until the beans are tender. Peel and chop the onion and garlic. Finely chop the hot pepper having carefully removed the seeds. De-seed and dice the green pepper. In a separate pan, heat the vegetable oil and fry the vegetables until soft. Add the bayleaves, oregano, ground cummin, pimento and black pepper. Stir in the black beans and their liquid and cook for a further 30 minutes. Add the sugar to the beans. Mix the cornflour with a tablespoon of cold water and stir into the stew. Cook, stirring for 5 minutes until the stew thickens.

Serves 4

Allow sufficient time to soak the beans as part of the preparation for this dish. This stew should be served with brown rice and accompanying vegetables.

Note: Be careful to wash hands and utensils after handling the hot pepper.

Ital Stew

Ingredients

1 lb (450 g) yam : 1 lb (450 g) pumpkin
1 lb (450 g) coco : ½ lb (225 g) cassava
½ lb (225 g) breadfruit
2 pt (1100 ml) vegetable stock
1 hot pepper : freshly ground black pepper
plain or cornmeal dumplings (see page 52)
3 green bananas : juice of ½ lime

Method

Remove the seeds from the pumpkin. Wash and peel the yam, pumpkin, coco and cassava. Slice the breadfruit into wedges, peel and cut out the heart. Chop all the vegetables into fairly large pieces. In a large pan bring the stock to the boil. Add the vegetables, the hot pepper and black pepper. Turn down the heat and simmer for 20 minutes. Meanwhile mix the dumplings. Add to the pan, turn up the heat and cook until the dumplings are done. In a separate pan boil the green bananas in their skins, having cut off both ends and split the skin deeply with a knife. When cooked, allow to cool a little before peeling. Cut each banana into three and add to the stew with the lime juice. Remove the hot pepper once the stew has reheated.

Serves 4–6

Serve this stew in a bowl with no accompaniment other than a simple salad.

Lentil Stew

Ingredients

8 oz (225 g) lentils or split peas
½ pt (275 ml) coconut milk
1 lb (450 g) pumpkin
2 medium-sized tomatoes
2 spring onions : 1 tsp pimento berries
1 sprig thyme : 1 hot pepper
freshly ground black pepper

Method

Cover the lentils or split peas with plenty of water, bring to the boil and simmer uncovered for 1 hour or until soft. Peel the pumpkin and remove the seeds. Dice. Blanch and peel the tomatoes and coarsely chop. Slice the spring onions. Crush the pimento berries and add these to the lentils with the vegetables, the whole hot pepper, thyme and black pepper. Add the coconut milk to the pan. Cook for a further 20–25 minutes until the pumpkin is tender. Remove the hot pepper before serving.

Serves 4

Unlike the other pulses lentils need no pre-soaking, and also act to thicken the stew. Serve this dish with rice and a side salad.

Millet and Spinach Stew

Ingredients

3 tbs vegetable oil
1 medium-sized onion
2 cloves of garlic
4 oz (115 g) millet grains
1 lb (450 g) spinach leaves
¾ pt (425 ml) vegetable stock
2 tbs peanut butter
freshly ground black pepper

Method

Place the vegetable oil in a pan over a medium heat. Peel and chop the onion and garlic and fry for 2–3 minutes. Stir in the millet grains, fry for a further 5–6 minutes. Carefully wash and chop the spinach and add to pan. Add the vegetable stock, peanut butter and black pepper. Stir well and simmer, covered, for 20–25 minutes.

Serves 4

Serve with vegetable accompaniments and a salad.

Stewed Ackees

(Pepperdash Stew)

Ingredients

1 medium-sized onion : 1 clove garlic
8 oz (225 g) tomatoes : 2 tbs vegetable oil
2–3 whole cloves : 1 hot pepper
1 large tin ackees (20 oz or 550 g) : juice of ½ lime
freshly ground black pepper
hot pepper sauce (optional)

Method

Peel the onion and slice into thin rings. Chop the garlic clove finely. Blanch the tomatoes, peel and coarsely chop. Heat the vegetable oil in a pan and fry the onion and garlic until softened. Add the chopped tomatoes, cloves and whole hot pepper and simmer gently for 7–8 minutes until the tomatoes have cooked down to a thickish sauce, stirring carefully so as not to break the whole hot pepper. Drain the ackees of most of their liquid and add to the pan with the lime juice and ground black pepper. Simmer for a further 10 minutes. Remove the hot pepper at the end of cooking and adjust seasoning to taste.

Serves 4

This dish is best served with a generous addition of hot pepper sauce, but, for the faint-hearted, it may be omitted. Serve with plain rice and plenty of iced water!

Vegetable Stew with Cornmeal Dumplings

Ingredients

3 tbs vegetable oil : 1 large onion
2 cloves of garlic : 1 leek
2 carrots : 2 medium-sized potatoes
1½ pts (850 ml) water : 2 bayleaves
1 sprig thyme : 1 hot pepper
4 pimento berries : ½ small cabbage
2 oz (55 g) creamed coconut : freshly ground black pepper
juice of ½ lime : cornmeal dumplings (see page 52)

Method

Heat the vegetable oil in a large saucepan. Peel and slice the onion, chop the garlic cloves, thoroughly wash and slice the leek. Cook the vegetables in the oil for 4–5 minutes until softened. Peel and chop the carrots and potatoes. Add to the pan with the water, bayleaves, thyme, whole hot pepper and pimento. Bring to the boil then turn down the heat and simmer for 15 minutes until the vegetables are just tender. Meanwhile mix the dumplings (see page 52). Roughly chop the cabbage and add to the pan, grate in the creamed coconut and drop in the dumplings one at a time. Add the lime juice and continue to cook the stew for a further 10 minutes until the dumplings are done. Remove the hot pepper before serving.

Serves 4–6

Serve in individual bowls with roti and a side salad.

Aubergine Stuffed with Cashew Nuts

(Uptown Garden Egg)

Ingredients

2 large aubergines : 2 tbs vegetable oil
2 medium-sized onions : 3 medium-sized tomatoes
4 oz (115 g) cashew nuts
freshly ground black pepper : 2 tbs parsley

Method

Bring a large pan of water to the boil and cook the aubergines whole for 10 minutes. Drain and allow to cool. Slice the aubergines in half lengthways and carefully scoop the flesh from the skins leaving a shell 1 cm thick. Reserve the skins and chop the flesh finely. Heat the oil in a frying pan. Peel and chop the onions and sauté in the oil for 3–4 minutes. Add the onions to the chopped aubergine. Peel and chop the tomatoes and roughly chop the cashew nuts. Stir these into the aubergine mixture and season with freshly ground black pepper and chopped parsley. Arrange the aubergine skins in a greased baking dish and fill with the nut mixture. Bake, covered with foil, in a pre-heated oven at 180 degrees C. (gas mark 4) for 20 minutes. Remove the cover and bake for a further 5 minutes.

Serves 4

The cashew nuts successfully compliment the nutty flavour of the aubergines and provide a surprising texture to the dish. Only the plain unsalted variety of cashews should be used. Serve with a salad or green vegetable.

Stuffed Red Peppers

Ingredients

4 large red peppers : 1 large onion
2 oz (55 g) fresh whole almonds
2–3 pimento berries
8 tbs fresh wholemeal breadcrumbs
2 oz (55 g) cooked peas : 1 oz (25 g) raisins
freshly ground black pepper
vegetable oil

Method

Blanch the peppers whole in boiling water for 5 minutes. Drain and cool under running cold water. Slice a lid from the stem end of each pepper and reserve. Remove seeds and white pith with a teaspoon. Peel and finely chop the onion. Blanch the almonds in boiling water, remove the skins and chop finely. Crush the pimento berries. Add these ingredients to the breadcrumbs and mix well. Stir in the cooked peas, raisins, black pepper and a little vegetable oil if the mixture seems dry. Stuff the peppers with the bread-crumb mixture and arrange in a greased oven-proof dish. Replace the lids on the peppers and secure with a skewer. Cover the dish and bake in a moderate oven at 180 degrees C. (gas mark 4) for 45–50 minutes.

Serves 4

Serve with vegetable accompaniment or a salad.

ACCOMPANIMENTS

Boiled Green Bananas

Buttered Sweet Potato

Celery and Rice

Fried Plantain

Mixed Greens

Rice and Peas

Roast Breadfruit

Steamed Cho Cho

Creole Sauce

Hot Pepper Sauce

Pumpkin Sauce

Boiled Green Bananas

Ingredients

4–6 green bananas

Method

Bring a large pan of water to the boil. Cut off both ends of the bananas and using a sharp knife score the banana skins deeply along their length. Either leave the bananas whole or cut in two crossways. Boil for 20 minutes until the bananas are soft. Drain. When cool enough to handle remove the skins and serve.

Serves 4

Slitting the green banana skins enables them to peel more easily when cooked.

Buttered Sweet Potato

Ingredients

2 lb (900 g) sweet potato
3–4 tbs peanut oil
2 oz (55 g) unsalted butter or vegetable margarine

Method

Wash, peel and thickly slice the sweet potato. Place the peanut oil in a heavy frying pan over a medium heat. Fry the sweet potato slices in the oil until golden brown and crisp (it may be necessary to do this in two batches). Slit each piece of sweet potato with a knife and spread the inside with a knob of butter or vegetable margarine.

Serves 4

Celery and Rice

Ingredients

2 sticks celery
2 slices fresh root ginger
2 tbs vegetable oil
8 oz (225 g) brown rice
1 bayleaf
½ tsp paprika

Method

Chop the celery. Peel and finely chop the fresh ginger. Heat the vegetable oil in a heavy based pan and fry the celery and ginger gently until the celery is soft. Wash the brown rice and drain thoroughly. Add the rice to the pan together with the bayleaf and sufficient cold water to cover the rice by 1–1½ cm. Bring to the boil then turn down the heat and simmer, uncovered, for twenty minutes until the rice is cooked and all the liquid has been absorbed. Sprinkle with paprika and serve.

Serves 4

Fried Plantain

Ingredients

3 ripe plantains
vegetable oil for frying

Method

Cut both ends off the plantains. Slit the skins lengthways right through to the flesh and prise off. Cut each plantain into three, crossways and then slice thickly along the length. Heat the vegetable oil in a heavy frying pan and fry the plantain slices until golden brown. Drain on kitchen paper and serve very hot.

Serves 4

Mixed Greens

Ingredients

1 lb (450 g) callaloo or spinach leaves
1 lb (450 g) cabbage : 1 large onion
1 hot pepper : 2 medium-sized tomatoes
1 spring onion : 2 tbs vegetable oil
1 tsp fresh thyme : freshly ground black pepper

Method

First carefully wash the callaloo or spinach. Drain and chop. Shred the cabbage, peel and slice the onion, de-seed and finely chop the hot pepper. Blanch the tomatoes, peel and chop and slice the spring onion. Heat the vegetable oil in a shallow pan, sauté the onion for two minutes before tossing in the greens, the finely chopped hot pepper, the tomatoes and spring onion. Season with thyme and black pepper. Reduce the heat to low and continue to cook, stirring occasionally until the vegetables are tender, about 15 minutes.

Serves 4

Note: Be careful to wash hands and utensils directly after preparing the hot pepper.

Rice and Peas

Ingredients

6 oz (170 g) gungo peas or black-eye beans
¼ pt (150 ml) coconut milk
8 oz (225 g) brown rice
1 sprig thyme
freshly ground black pepper

Method

Soak the dried peas or beans in plenty of cold water overnight. Drain. Place in a pan with enough cold water to cover. Bring to the boil, cover and simmer for ¾–1 hour until the peas are tender. Add the washed rice to the pan together with the coconut milk and a seasoning of thyme and freshly ground black pepper. Add extra water to bring the level of liquid in the pan 1–2 cm above the rice. Cook on a low heat for a further 20–25 minutes by which time all the liquid should be absorbed and the rice soft.

Serves 4

Note: This dish needs to be started the night before to allow for soaking times.

Roast Breadfruit

Ingredients

1 firm breadfruit
2 oz (55 g) unsalted butter or vegetable margarine

Method

Wash and dry the breadfruit. Using a small sharp knife cut out the stem of the breadfruit and reserve. Hollow out a little more of the heart of the breadfruit, cutting as deeply as possible. Pack the cavity with the unsalted butter or vegetable margarine and replace the stem as a lid. Wrap the whole breadfruit in aluminium foil. Preheat the oven to 200 degrees C. (gas mark 6) and bake the breadfruit for 50–60 minutes until it can easily be pierced by a knife or skewer. Remove the foil. Carefully slice the hot breadfruit into wedges and peel. Cut out the core and arrange the wedges on a warm plate. Dot with a little more butter and serve.

Serves 8

Creole Sauce

Ingredients

1 medium-sized onion : ½ green pepper
2 tbs vegetable oil : ½ lb (225 g) tomatoes
1 hot pepper
¼ pt (150 ml) water or vegetable stock
1 tsp lime juice : 1 tsp vinegar
freshly ground black pepper
fresh coriander leaves

Method

Peel and chop the onion. Remove the seeds from the green pepper and dice. Heat the vegetable oil in a saucepan and sauté the onion and pepper until they are soft. Blanch, peel and coarsely chop the tomatoes. De-seed and chop the hot pepper. Add these and all remaining ingredients, except the coriander, to the pan. Bring to the boil, turn down the heat and simmer for 15 minutes until the sauce becomes thick. Cool slightly, then purée in an electric blender or food processor until smooth. Reheat and serve sprinkled with chopped fresh coriander.

Note: Hands and utensils should be washed directly after preparing the hot pepper.

Hot Pepper Sauce

Ingredients

1 large onion
2 shallots or spring onions
1 tbs lime juice
12 hot peppers
2 cloves garlic
2 tbs vegetable oil

Method

Peel and chop the onions and shallots. Mix with the lime juice and leave to stand for 1 hour. Carefully remove the seeds from the hot peppers and chop. Crush the cloves of garlic. Combine all the ingredients in a small saucepan and bring to the boil. Simmer covered on a low heat until the mixture is thick, about 15–20 minutes. Serve straight away or cool and bottle.

Note: Thoroughly wash hands and utensils after preparing the hot peppers.

Pumpkin Sauce

Ingredients

½ lb (225 g) pumpkin
¾ pt (425 ml) boiling water
2 tsp cornflour
¼ pt (150 ml) coconut milk
freshly grated nutmeg

Method

Wash and peel the pumpkin. Roughly chop, add to the boiling water in a pan and cook until tender. Cool slightly, blend the pumpkin with the water in a liquidizer or food processor. Return to the pan. Mix the cornflour with the coconut milk and add to the pumpkin mixture. Cook gently, stirring until the sauce thickens. Season with a grating of nutmeg.

SALADS

Avocado Salad

Bean and Pepper Salad

Beansprout Salad

Breadfruit Mayonnaise

Cabbage and Carrot Salad

Carrot and Raisin Salad

Fresh Orange Salad

Jamaican Salad

Lentil Salad

Pineapple, Banana and Tofu Salad

Rice Salad

Sweet Pepper and Pineapple Salad

Avocado Salad

Ingredients

1 large ripe avocado
2 tsp lime juice
1 medium-sized onion
3 medium-sized tomatoes
¼ cabbage or whole chinese leaf

Method

Cut the avocado lengthways into thick slices. Remove the stone and skin, then sprinkle the lime juice over the slices. Peel the onion and slice into fine rings. Slice the tomatoes. Wash the cabbage or chinese leaf, drain and shred finely. Arrange a bed of shredded cabbage on a serving plate, top with the avocado slices and garnish with tomato and onion. Serve immediately.

Serves 4

Bean and Pepper Salad

(Rasta Salad)

Ingredients

4 oz (115 g) red kidney beans
4 oz (115 g) black-eyed beans
1 red pepper : 1 green pepper
1 yellow pepper : 4 tbs peanut oil
1 tsp vinegar : juice of 1 lime
freshly ground black pepper

Method

Soak the kidney beans and black-eyed beans separately in plenty of cold water overnight. In separate saucepans cover the beans with fresh water, bring to the boil and simmer for 1 hour until they are soft. Drain and cool. Cut off the stem end of the peppers and scoop out the seeds, slice the peppers into thin rings. Mix the dressing ingredients, the oil, the vinegar, lime juice and black pepper, beating with a fork. Combine the beans in a serving dish and pour over the dressing. Arrange the peppers on top of the beans.

Serves 4

A beautifully coloured salad, the red and white of the beans topped by the symbolic red, gold and green of the peppers. Preparations need to begin a day in advance to allow time for soaking the beans.

Beansprout Salad

Ingredients

3 oz (85 g) mung or aduki beansprouts
3 oz (85 g) alfalfa sprouts
3 oz (85 g) cooked sweetcorn
2 sticks celery
3 tbs peanut oil
1 tbs lime juice
freshly ground black pepper
2 tsp sesame seeds

Method

Mix the beansprouts, alfalfa sprouts and sweetcorn in a salad bowl. Finely slice the celery and add to the beansprouts. Beat the lime juice and peanut oil together, season with black pepper. In a pre-heated moderate oven 180 degrees C. (gas mark 4) roast the sesame seeds on a baking tray until lightly coloured. When ready to serve pour the dressing over the salad and sprinkle with sesame seeds.

Serves 4

Breadfruit Mayonnaise

Ingredients

½ large roast breadfruit
¼ pt (150 ml) mayonnaise
2 tsp soured cream or yoghurt
¼ tsp ground cinnamon
3 oz (85 g) shelled raw peanuts

Method

Peel the breadfruit, remove the core and dice or cut into slices. Beat the mayonnaise and soured cream or yoghurt together and flavour with ground cinnamon. Toast the peanuts under a hot grill until lightly coloured. Mix the breadfruit with the mayonnaise and arrange in a serving dish. Sprinkle with the toasted nuts.

Serves 4

Eggless or soya-based alternatives may be used in place of ordinary mayonnaise. This recipe works equally well with yams.

Carrot and Raisin Salad

Ingredients

4 oz (115 g) raisins
¼ pt (150 ml) orange juice
1 lb (450 g) carrots
3–4 slices fresh root ginger

Method

Soak the raisins in the orange juice for 1 hour or until plump. Wash, peel and grate the carrots. Peel and grate or finely chop the root ginger. Toss all the ingredients together until well mixed.

Serves 4

An unusual salad of grated carrots and ginger sweetened by the addition of raisins.

Cabbage and Carrot Salad

(Ital Coleslaw)

Ingredients

½ cabbage or whole chinese leaf
½ cucumber
2 medium-sized carrots
3 medium-sized tomatoes
3 oz (85 g) beansprouts
3 tbs sunflower oil
1 tbs vinegar
freshly ground black pepper

Method

Wash the cabbage or chinese leaf, drain and shred finely. Wash and thinly slice the cucumber, peel and grate the carrots and slice the tomatoes. Arrange the shredded cabbage on a serving dish. Edge the dish with slices of cucumber. Combine the grated carrots and beansprouts in a bowl. Mix the dressing ingredients – oil, vinegar, and black pepper – beating with a fork until well blended, then pour over the carrots and beansprouts. Toss together and arrange in the centre of the dish. Decorate with sliced tomatoes.

Serves 4

Fresh Orange Salad

(Smile Orange)

Ingredients

5–6 large oranges
raw cane sugar
¼ tsp ground cinnamon

Method

Blanch the oranges in boiling water for 1 minute. This will enable you to remove the skin without damaging the oranges. Cut the fruit into thin slices, removing any pips. Arrange the slices on a serving dish and chill. Serve sprinkled with raw cane sugar and cinnamon.

Serves 4

A light refreshing salad to serve with a substantial main course.

Jamaican Salad

Ingredients

¼ cabbage
1 crisp lettuce
4 slices fresh pineapple
¼ fresh coconut
4 tbs pineapple juice

Method

Remove the tough outer leaves from the cabbage. Wash the cabbage and lettuce, drain and shred finely. Peel the coconut and chop into small pieces. Cube the pineapple. Combine all the ingredients in a bowl, pour over the pineapple juice and serve.

Serves 4

Lentil Salad

Ingredients

8 oz (225 g) whole green or brown lentils
4 tbs peanut oil
1 tbs lime juice
freshly ground black pepper
3–4 fresh chilli peppers
6 shallots
1 lime for garnishing

Method

Place the washed lentils in a saucepan with plenty of cold water. Bring to the boil and simmer until cooked for about one and a half hours. Drain and cool. Mix the oil, lime juice and black pepper to make a dressing. Cut the stem from the chilli peppers, slit them and carefully remove the seeds. Peel and chop the shallots. Place the cooked lentils in a large bowl, add the chillies and shallots and the dressing. Mix thoroughly and chill before serving. Garnish with slices of lime.

Serves 4

Note: Be careful to wash hands and utensils after contact with the chilli peppers.

Pineapple, Banana and Tofu Salad

Ingredients

4 slices fresh pineapple
4 oz (115 g) tofu
3 ripe bananas
2 tbs pineapple juice
1 tsp clear honey
5–6 crisp lettuce leaves

Method

Cut the fresh pineapple into diced pieces. Cut the tofu into cubes the same size as the pineapple. Peel the bananas and cut diagonally into slices 1 cm thick. Mix the pineapple juice and honey until well blended. Combine all the salad ingredients into a bowl lined with lettuce leaves. Pour on the dressing and serve.

Serves 4

A fruit and soya bean curd salad, the flavours go surprisingly well together.

Rice Salad

Ingredients

8 oz (225 g) cooked brown rice
1 medium-sized onion
2 sticks celery
1 green pepper
3 oz (85 g) roasted cashew nuts
1 clove garlic
4 tbs tomato juice

Method

Place the cooked brown rice in a large serving dish. Peel and chop the onion, slice the celery, de-seed and dice the green pepper. Mix the chopped vegetables into the rice and add the cashew nuts which have been lightly roasted in a moderate oven or under a hot grill. Crush the garlic clove and add to the tomato juice. When ready to serve, pour the dressing over the salad and toss.

Serves 4

An excellent way to use left over brown rice, combining it with crunchy vegetables and nuts and a delicious garlicky dressing.

Sweet Pepper and Pineapple Salad

Ingredients

1 crisp lettuce
4 slices fresh pineapple
½ cucumber
1 red pepper
2–3 spring onions

Method

Wash the lettuce, drain and shred. Dice the pineapple and cucumber. De-seed the red pepper and slice into strips. Slice the spring onions. Line a serving plate with the lettuce. Combine the pineapple, red pepper, cucumber and spring onions and arrange on top of the lettuce.

Serves 4

DESSERTS

Baked Bananas

Grilled Bananas

Coconut Tart

Mango Cream

Cassava Pone

Dokono

Steamed Groundnut Pudding

Banana Ice-cream

Mango Ice-cream

Paw Paw Ice-cream

Soya Bean Ice-cream

Custard Sauce

Baked Bananas

Ingredients

4 large ripe bananas
2 oz (55 g) unsalted butter or vegetable margarine
1–2 tbs clear honey
4 tbs lime or orange juice
½ tsp pimento berries

Method

Peel the bananas and slice into two lengthways. Use a little of the butter to grease a shallow oven proof dish and arrange the bananas in it. Mix together the honey, lime or orange juice, and crush the pimento berries using a pestle and mortar. Pour the fruit juice mixture over the banana slices, sprinkle with the crushed pimento and dot with remaining butter. Bake at 200 degrees C. (gas mark 4) for 15–20 minutes.

Serves 4

A simple dish of bananas baked with fruit juice and honey.

Grilled Bananas

Ingredients

4 large firm bananas
1 large lime
maple syrup

Method

Keeping on the skins, slit the bananas lengthways down one side through to the flesh. Preheat the grill and grill until they are charred and soft, turning them over a few times. Remove the skins carefully so as not to break the bananas. Serve with wedges of lime and maple syrup.

Serves 4

Coconut Tart

Ingredients

6 oz (170 g) wholemeal flour : ½ tsp baking powder
3 oz (85 g) unsalted butter or vegetable margarine
1 mature coconut : 3 slices fresh root ginger
8 oz (225 g) raw cane sugar
½ tsp freshly grated root ginger
4–5 drops vanilla essence

Method

First make the shortcrust pastry. Sift the flour and baking powder into a bowl and rub in the butter or vegetable margarine with the fingers. Add cold water a tablespoon at a time and blend until the ingredients form a soft, but not sticky, dough. Knead briefly on a floured surface and let the pastry rest in a cool place while the filling is made. Peel and grate the coconut and the ginger and combine with the sugar in a heavy based saucepan. Heat gently until the sugar dissolves, then boil rapidly on a high heat stirring constantly until most of the liquid evaporates and the coconut takes on a translucent appearance. (The mixture should be moist but not wet.) Flavour with nutmeg and vanilla. Roll out the pastry and use to line an 8-inch (20 cm) tart or pie dish. Fill with the coconut and bake in a pre-heated oven at 200 degrees C. (gas mark 4) for about 20 minutes until the pastry is lightly coloured.

Serves 6

Another favourite recipe from my father's repertoire.

Mango Cream

Ingredients

1½ lb (675 g) mangoes
2 tbs cornflour or arrowroot powder
1 pt (550 ml) soya milk
honey or maple syrup

Method

Peel the ripe mangoes and slice the flesh off the stone, reserving some slices for decoration. Puree the remaining mango in an electric blender and pass through a sieve. Heat the soya milk to near boiling point over a gentle heat. Meanwhile mix the cornflour or arrowroot with a little water in a bowl. Pour on the hot milk, mix well and return to the saucepan briefly, stirring until the mixture thickens. Leave to cool. Combine the mango purée and the cornflour or arrowroot custard and mix, sweeten with clear honey or maple syrup. Spoon into individual bowls and chill. Serve garnished with slices of fresh mango.

Serves 4

A smooth delicious cream. The honey or maple syrup give an added sweetness to the scented flavour of the mangoes.

Cassava Pone

Ingredients

2 lb (900 g) sweet cassava
1 mature coconut
½ tsp grated nutmeg
5–6 drops vanilla essence
6 oz (170 g) raw cane sugar
1 pt (550 ml) milk

Method

Peel and grate the cassava and coconut. Combine in a bowl with the freshly grated nutmeg, vanilla essence and sugar. Stir in the milk to form a soft thick batter. Pour the mixture into a well-greased baking dish and bake in a preheated moderate oven at 180 degrees C. (gas mark 4) for 1 to 1¼ hours or until set.

Serves 6

This recipe does require a bit of effort in grating the two main ingredients, the cassava and coconut, but the end result is well worth the time involved.

Dokono

(Blue Drawers)

Ingredients

8 oz (225 g) cornmeal
4 oz (115 g) raw cane sugar
¾ pt (425 ml) coconut milk
½ tsp ground cinnamon
4–5 drops vanilla essence
3 oz (85 g) raisins

Method

Mix together the cornmeal and the sugar in a bowl. Pour in the coconut milk and stir well to produce a smooth consistency. Flavour with ground cinnamon and vanilla essence and stir in the raisins. Drop the mixture in heaped tablespoons on to 6 inch (15 cm) squares of aluminium foil. Fold the foil to make parcels of the mixture and press the edges well to seal. Bring a large pan of water to the boil and cook the dokono parcels in the boiling water for 1 hour. At the end of the cooking time carefully remove the foil and serve the dokono hot, sprinkled with a little sugar.

Serves four

Common to several Caribbean Islands, this dish is of African origin. The authentic version would be cooked wrapped in banana leaves for which aluminium foil is a modern if not quite aesthetic substitute.

Steamed Groundnut Pudding

(Dread Nut Pudding)

Ingredients

4 oz (115 g) shelled peanuts or groundnuts
4 oz (115 g) cornmeal or wholemeal flour
2 tsp baking powder
4 oz (115 g) raw cane sugar
¼ pt (150 ml) milk

Method

Place the shelled peanuts or groundnuts in an electric blender and grind until fine. Mix with the cornmeal or wholemeal flour and the baking powder. Add the raw cane sugar and stir in the milk. Mix until well blended. Pour the mixture into a greased pudding basin, cover tightly with aluminium foil and secure with string. Half fill a large saucepan with water and bring to the boil. Carefully lower the pudding basin into the pan (the water should not come much more than halfway up the sides of the basin). Cover the pan and steam the pudding on a low heat for two hours.

Serves 4

A recipe from Ethiopia. It is delicious served hot with honey or fresh fruit.

Sweet Potato Pudding

Ingredients

1 lb (450 g) sweet potato : 3 slices fresh root ginger
1 oz (25 g) unsalted butter or vegetable margarine
8 oz (225 g) raw cane sugar
¼ tsp freshly grated nutmeg
¼ tsp ground cinnamon : 4–5 drops vanilla essence
½ pt (257 ml) coconut milk
wholemeal flour : 3 oz (85 g) raisins

Method

Peel and grate the sweet potato and the fresh root ginger. Mix in the butter or vegetable margarine, the sugar, spices and vanilla essence. Stir in the coconut milk and enough wholemeal flour to bind the mixture producing a stiff batter. Finally mix in the raisins. Grease a shallow oven-proof dish, pour in the sweet potato mixture and bake in a preheated oven at 180 degrees C. (gas mark 4) for 1¼ hours.

Serves 6

A rich moist pudding flavoured with ginger and sweet spices.

Basic Custard for Ice-Cream

Ingredients

2 tbs arrowroot powder
1 pt (550 ml) milk
¼ pt (150 ml) evaporated milk AND 4 oz (115 g) raw cane sugar
OR ¼ pt (150 ml) condensed milk

Method

Mix the arrowroot with a little of the milk. Heat the rest of the milk in a saucepan and when it reaches boiling point stir in the arrowroot mixture and cook gently for 3 minutes until thickened. Remove from the heat, cool slightly and mix in the evaporated milk and sugar OR the condensed milk. Keep stirring until the sugar has dissolved. Add the fruit puree (see following recipes) to the custard and pour into a freezer container. Place in the refrigerator until cold and then transfer to the freezer. After 1 hour take out of the freezer and beat vigorously with a fork to break up the large ice crystals. Repeat the process after a further hour and twice more at 30 minute intervals.

Banana Ice Cream

Method

Substitute the evaporated milk and sugar with ¼ pt (150 ml) peanut milk made by liquidizing 3 oz (85 kg) shelled roasted peanuts with ¼ pt (150 ml) water. Strain this mixture through a sieve lined with muslin and sweeten with honey. Purée or mash 3–4 ripe bananas to a smooth paste. Add to the cooled custard and freeze as directed.

Coconut Ice Cream

Method

Substitute half the milk with coconut milk made from 1 large coconut, grated and ¾ pt (425 ml) warm water. Having mixed the grated coconut and warm water, strain through a muslin cloth, squeezing to extract all the juice. Follow the instructions for the basic custard and freeze.

Mango Ice Cream

Method

Make ½ pt (275 ml) mango purée by liquidizing the flesh in an electric blender and straining through a sieve. Add the purée to the basic custard and freeze.

Paw Paw Ice Cream

Method

Peel the paw paw, halve and remove the seeds. Blend or mash to make ½ pt (275 ml) of fruit purée. Add this to the basic custard and freeze as directed.

Soya Bean Ice Cream

Method

Replace the arrowroot with 2 oz (55 g) soya bean powder. Make up double the quantity of peanut milk (as given for Banana Ice Cream) and substitute for the evaporated milk. Include the raw cane sugar for this recipe. Boil the custard until it thickens and set to freeze according to the directions given.

Custard Sauce

Ingredients

3 tbs cornflour
¾ pt (425 ml) coconut milk
2 tbs raw cane sugar

Method

Blend the cornflour and sugar with a little milk or water. Bring the coconut milk to boiling point in a saucepan, pour in the cornflour mixture and simmer for 5 minutes stirring constantly as the custard thickens.

Serves 4

An 'Ital' alternative to egg-based custard.

PORRIDGE

Banana Porridge

Cornmeal Porridge

Corn Porridge

Banana Porridge

Ingredients

3 green bananas
1 pt (550 ml) water
½ pt (275 ml) coconut milk
½ tsp ground cinnamon
½ tsp freshly grated nutmeg
2 tbs wholemeal flour
milk or water
raw cane sugar

Method

Peel the green bananas by slicing off both ends then splitting them lengthways cutting through to the flesh and prising off the skins. Grate or blend the bananas in an electric blender. Beat in the water and coconut milk until the mixture is smooth. Pour into a saucepan. Over a gentle heat bring the pan to the boil and simmer for 15–20 minutes until the mixture is cooked. Add the cinnamon, nutmeg and the wholemeal flour which should be blended to a thin paste with a little milk or water. Stir while the porridge thickens and cook for a further 10 minutes. Serve in bowls thickly sprinkled with raw cane sugar.

Serves 4

Here green bananas are used to make an 'Ital' breakfast dish flavoured with sweet spices.

Cornmeal Porridge

Ingredients

6 oz (170 g) cornmeal
1½ pt (850 ml) milk
1 stick of cinnamon (5 cm)
½ tsp freshly grated nutmeg
raw cane sugar

Method

Mix the cornmeal and milk thoroughly in a saucepan, place over a medium heat and bring to the boil, stirring constantly until smooth and thick. Lower the heat, add the spices and flavouring of vanilla essence. Sweeten to taste with raw cane sugar. Continue to cook for a further 10–12 minutes stirring occasionally. Remove the cinnamon stick before serving.

Serves 4

A delicious porridge which is very easy to make.

Corn Porridge

Ingredients

8 oz (225 g) hominy corn
1 pt (550 ml) water
1 pt (550 ml) coconut milk
2 tbs cornflour
1 stick of cinnamon (5 cm)
½ tsp freshly grated nutmeg
½ tsp rosewater
raw cane sugar

Method

Wash the corn, place in a pan with the water and boil until soft. Mix the coconut milk with the cornflour and pour into the pan. Cook stirring continuously as the mixture thickens. Add the spices and rosewater and simmer for 15–20 minutes, giving the porridge the occasional stir. Sweeten to taste with raw cane sugar.

Serves 4

BREAD AND CAKES

Banana and Soya Loaf

Molasses and Cornmeal Bread

Pumpkin Bread

Coconut Buns

Grater Cakes

Ital Banana Cake

Ground Rice Cake

Banana and Soya Loaf

Ingredients

6 oz (170 g) wholemeal flour
3 oz (85 g) soya flour
2 tsp baking powder
4 oz (115 g) vegetable margarine
3 oz (85 g) raw cane sugar
3 large ripe bananas
2 oz (55 g) cashew or pecan nuts

Method

Sift the flour, soya flour and baking powder together. Cream the margarine and raw cane sugar until well blended. Peel the ripe bananas and mash well with a fork to make a thick purée. Mix the bananas into the creamed mixture and gradually stir in the sifted ingredients. Roughly chop the cashew or pecan nuts and add. Grease and line a 2 lb loaf tin and pour in the banana mixture. Preheat the oven to 180 degrees C. (gas mark 4) and bake the loaf for about 1 hour until well risen and golden brown.

The bananas used in this recipe can be puréed in an electric blender or food processor, but the resulting texture is disappointing compared to the hand method. The moist bread can be served on its own or spread with unsalted butter or vegetable margarine.

Molasses and Cornmeal Bread

Ingredients

6 oz (170 g) cornmeal
2 oz (55 g) wholemeal flour
4 tsp baking powder
¼ tsp freshly grated nutmeg
¼ tsp ground cinnamon
4 oz (115 g) vegetable margarine
2 tbs molasses : 2 tbs milk
4 oz (115 g) grated coconut

Method

Sift the cornmeal, flour, baking powder and spices together in a bowl. Melt the vegetable margarine and molasses in a saucepan and pour on to the dry ingredients. Stir in the milk and grated coconut. Mix well. Pour the mixture into a greased 2 lb loaf tin. Heat the oven to 180 degrees C. (gas mark 4) and bake the bread for 35–40 minutes until well risen.

The relatively large amount of baking powder in this recipe is needed to compensate for the heaviness of the cornmeal.

Pumpkin Bread

Ingredients

8 oz (225 g) wholemeal flour
3 tsp baking powder
4 oz (115 g) vegetable margarine
4 oz (115 g) raw cane sugar
½ lb (225 g) cooked pumpkin
2–3 tbs milk
3 oz (85 g) raisins
½ tsp freshly grated nutmeg

Method

Sift the flour and baking powder. Cream the margarine and sugar together in a bowl. Mash the cooked pumpkin until smooth and add to the creamed mixture. Fold in the sifted ingredients and moisten with the milk. Finally stir in the nutmeg and raisins. Spoon the mixture into a greased 2 lb loaf tin and bake for 35–40 minutes at 180 degrees C. (gas mark 4).

Coconut Buns

Ingredients

4 oz (115 g) vegetable margarine
6 oz (170 g) raw cane sugar
10 oz (280 g) wholemeal flour
2 tsp baking powder
½ tsp ground cinnamon
6 oz (170 g) freshly grated coconut
¼ pt (150 ml) milk

Method

Cream the margarine and raw cane sugar until well blended. Sift the flour, baking powder and ground cinnamon in a separate bowl. Stir in the grated coconut. Add the dry ingredients alternately with the milk to the creamed mixture, mixing it thoroughly to produce a thick dough-like consistency. Divide the mixture and shape into buns with floured hands. Place the buns on a greased baking sheet, spacing them well apart, and bake in a preheated oven at 180 degrees C. (gas mark 4) until risen and brown.

Makes 8–10

Delicious spicy buns. Freshly grated coconut should be used in preference to the non-Ital dessicated kind.

Grater Cakes

Ingredients

1 large coconut
3–4 slices fresh root ginger
1½ pt (850 ml) water
1 lb (450 g) raw cane sugar

Method

Peel and grate the coconut and the peeled fresh ginger. Pour the water into a large heavy based saucepan, add the coconut and ginger and simmer on a low heat until the water is reduced to about ½ pt (275 ml). Add the raw cane sugar and once dissolved boil hard stirring continuously until the mixture becomes thick and, if a little is dropped into cold water, will harden immediately. Drop spoonfuls of this on to a lightly oiled tray and allow to cool.

Makes 18–20

Ital Banana Cake

Ingredients

4 oz (115 g) vegetable margarine
3 large ripe bananas
2 tbs clear honey
8 oz (225 g) wholemeal flour
2 tsp baking powder
½ tsp freshly grated nutmeg
4–5 drops vanilla essence
2 oz (55 g) cashew nuts

Method

Cream the margarine until soft. Peel the bananas. Slice 9 diagonal slices from one of the bananas and reserve. Mash the remaining bananas with a fork and beat this purée into the margarine with the honey. Sift the wholemeal flour and baking powder and fold into the mixture. Add the freshly grated nutmeg, the vanilla essence and finally stir in the raisins and roughly chopped cashew nuts. Grease an 8-inch (20 cm) square cake tin. Spoon in the banana mixture and spread evenly. Using the point of a knife lightly mark the surface of the cake into 9 equal squares. Centre a slice of banana in each square. Bake in a preheated oven at 180 degrees C. (gas mark 4) for 35–40 minutes. Cool and slice into 9 square pieces.

Ground Rice Cake

Ingredients

4 oz (115 g) vegetable margarine
6 oz (170 g) raw cane sugar
4 oz (115 g) wholemeal flour
2 tsp baking powder
4 oz (115 g) ground rice
4–5 tbs milk
grated rind of 1 orange
1 tsp rosewater

Method

Cream together the margarine and the sugar. Sift the flour, baking powder and ground rice. Add the dry ingredients to the creamed mixture alternating with the milk to form a soft, but not wet consistency. Stir in the orange rind and the rosewater and mix well. Turn the mixture into a greased cake tin and bake in a preheated oven at 180 degrees C. (gas mark 4) for 1 hour.

This cake has a moist texture and unusual flavouring of orange and rosewater.

Glossary of Terms

Ackee
The fruit of a West African tree introduced to Jamaica by the British. When ripe, the scarlet shell of the ackee splits open to reveal three shiny black seeds surrounded by three segments of edible flesh. The flesh is cooked and served as a vegetable which has a delicate flavour. Fresh ackees are rarely available in Britain, is readily available in tins.

Aubergine
Also known as Eggplant or Belangere, it comes in a variety of sizes and colours, the most common being a deep-purple. It is cooked and eaten as a vegetable.

Avocado
First cultivated in Mexico but now common in most tropical countries. Avocados range from the black wrinkled-skin varieties to the large, green, smooth-skinned types. They are pear-like in shape with a large stone at the centre. The flesh is yellow/green with a buttery texture. Usually sold unripe, they should be kept until the fruit gives a little when gently squeezed. Once cut, the flesh should be sprinkled with lime juice to prevent discolouring.

Banana
A fully ripe banana has no tinges of green and the yellow skin is slightly speckled. Unripe green bananas are cooked and eaten as a starchy vegetable. Boiled with the skin on, both ends of green banana should be clipped and the skin deeply scored with a knife along its length to enable easy removal.

Breadfruit
A large, round, green-skinned fruit cooked as a vegetable. The creamy white flesh has a starchy texture. The central woody core is inedible and should be removed prior to serving.

Callaloo
Originally from Africa, the name refers to the leaves of the taro plant. Pak choy (Chinese spinach) or fresh leaf spinach may be substituted if fresh callaloo is not available.

Cassava
A tropical plant with a long tuberous root covered with bark-like, hairy skin. When peeled, the flesh is white and hard. Cassava is eaten as a vegetable or made into flour for cakes and bread.

Cho cho
Also known as Christophene, the cho cho closely resembles a pear in shape, with a slightly prickly skin, colour ranges from pale green to white. It is boiled and eaten as a vegetable.

Coco
Otherwise known as Eddo or Taro, this is a hairy tuber about the size of a potato. When peeled the flesh is pink or white in colour.

Coconut
Nut of the coconut tree – when buying choose coconuts which are heavy and contain liquid (shake to verify).

Coconut milk
Made by adding the flesh (grated) from one coconut to about 1 pt/550 ml of water. After mixing the liquid is then strained through muslin cloth to extract all the juice. The process may be repeated before the coconut is discarded.

Ginger
A knobbly root with a papery brown skin and moist yellow flesh which has a sharp pungent flavour.

Lime
A citrus fruit, small and round with a bright yellow or green skin. The juice is sharper and has a more distinct flavour than that of the lemon.

Mango
The mango tree is native to Asia but is now widely cultivated in the tropics. The fruits come in different shapes and sizes, the skin ranging in colour when ripe from green to deep red, with flesh tinted yellow to orange. Mangoes have a delicate fragrance and a sweet taste.

Nutmeg
A dark-brown nut added as a spice to both sweet and savoury food. The flavour is far superior when freshly grated.

Okra
Introduced into the Caribbean from Africa, although of tropical Asian origin, it is also known as Ladies' Fingers. The pods are green and tapered and should be eaten young. The principal ingredient in the dish Gumbo, Okra has a rather slimy texture when cooked.

Pawpaw
Also called papaya, the long oval fruits are hard and green when unripe. At this stage they are often cooked as a vegetable. When ripe they are yellow/orange in colour and slightly soft. The flesh inside is yellow or coral-coloured and the centre filled with small black seeds.

Peanut Milk
To make peanut milk, remove shell and inner skin of the peanuts and blend 4 oz/115 g (unshelled weight) with ½ pt/275 ml water. Strain through muslin and sweeten with honey.

Pepper
Both the sweet bell-peppers or capsicums, and the hot peppers originated from Mexico. The hot peppers of the Caribbean, sometimes called Scotch Bonnet peppers because of their wrinkled appearance, may be pale green, yellow, orange, or red. The seeds are best removed to reduce the fiery taste.

Pimento
Also known as Allspice or Jamaican Pepper, it is the dried berry of a tree native to Jamaica. Closely resembling peppercorns, the pimento has the combined flavour of nutmeg, cinnamon and cloves.

Pineapple
Perhaps the most popular tropical fruit. When ripe, it should give slightly when pressed.

Plantain
A member of the banana family, the plantain is only eaten cooked, ripe or unripe. When green, the thick skin of the plantain is difficult to remove.

Sweet Potato
Round or elongated tubers native to South America. The skin is reddish brown, pink or white, the flesh ranges from yellow to white and is slightly sweet.

Yam
There are several varieties of this edible tuber (Yellow yam, Negro yam, etc.) and the size and shape vary enormously. When peeled of its thick tough skin, the flesh is yellow or white (occasionally purple) with a nut-like flavour. It is boiled and eaten as a vegetable.